Gays and Mental Health: Fighting Depression, Saying No to Suicide

The Gallup's Guide to Modern Gay, Lesbian, & Transgender Lifestyle

Gays and Mental Health: Fighting Depression, Saying No to Suicide

by Jaime A. Seba

Mason Crest Publishers

MASON CREST PUBLISHERS INC.
370 Reed Road
Broomall, Pennsylvania 19008
(866)MCP-BOOK (toll free)
www.masoncrest.com

First Printing
9 8 7 6 5 4 3 2 1

Library of Congress Cataloging-in-Publication Data
Seba, Jaime.
 Gays and mental health : fighting depression, saying no to suicide / by Jaime A. Seba.
    p. cm.— (The Gallup's guide to modern gay, lesbian, & transgender lifestyle)
 Includes bibliographical references and index.
 ISBN 978-1-4222-1751-1 (hardcover) ISBN 978-1-4222-1758-0 (series)
 ISBN 978-1-4222-1870-9 (pbk.)   ISBN 978-1-4222-1863-1 (pbk series)
 1. Gays—Mental health. 2. Gays—Psychology. 3. Depression, Mental. 4. Gays—Suicidal behavior. I. Title.
 RC451.4.G39S43 2011
 616.890086'64—dc22
                              2010021838

Produced by Harding House Publishing Service, Inc.
www.hardinghousepages.com
Interior design by MK Bassett-Harvey.
Cover design by Torque Advertising + Design.
Printed in the USA by Bang Printing

Contents

PICTURE CREDITS

Introduction

We are both individuals and community members. Our differences define individuality; our commonalities create a community. Some differences, like the ability to run swiftly or to speak confidently, can make an individual stand out in a way that is viewed as beneficial by a community, while the group may frown upon others. Some of those differences may be difficult to hide (like skin color or physical disability), while others can be hidden (like religious views or sexual orientation). Moreover, what some communities or cultures deem as desirable differences, like thinness, is a negative quality in other contemporary communities. This is certainly the case with sexual orientation and gender identity, as explained in *Homosexuality Around the World*, one of the volumes in this book series.

Often, there is a tension between the individual (individual rights) and the community (common good). This is easily visible in everyday matters like the right to own land versus the common good of building roads. These cases sometimes result in community controversy and often are adjudicated by the courts.

An even more basic right than property ownership, however, is one's gender and sexuality. Does the right of gender expression trump the concerns and fears of a community or a family or a school? *Feeling Wrong in Your Own Body*, as the author of that volume suggests, means confronting, in the most personal way, the tension between individuality and community. And, while a community, family, and school have the right (and obligation) to protect its children, does the notion of property rights extend to controlling young adults' choice as to how they express themselves in terms of gender or sexuality?

Changes in how a community (or a majority of the community) thinks about an individual right or responsibility often precedes changes in the law enacted by legislatures or decided by courts. And for these changes to occur, individuals (sometimes working in small groups) often defied popular opinion, political pressure, or religious beliefs. Some of these trends are discussed in *A New Generation of Homosexuality*. Every generation (including yours!) stands on the accomplishments of our ancestors and in *Gay and Lesbian Role Models* you'll be reading about some of them.

One of the most pernicious aspects of discrimination on the basis of sexual orientation is that "homosexuality" is a stigma that can be hidden (see the volume about *Homophobia*). While some of my generation (I was your age in the early 1960s) think that life is so much easier being "queer" in the age of the Internet, Gay-Straight Alliances, and Ellen, in reality, being different in areas where difference matters is *always* difficult. Coming Out, as described in the volume of the same title, is always challenging—for both those who choose to come out and for the friends and family they trust with what was once a hidden truth. Being healthy means being honest—at least to yourself. Having supportive friends and family is most important, as explained in *Being Gay, Staying Healthy*.

Sometimes we create our own "families"—persons bound together by love and identity but not by name or bloodline. This is quite common in gay communities today as it was several generations ago. Forming families or small communities based on rejection by the larger community can also be a double-edged sword. While these can be positive, they may also turn into prisons of conformity. Does being lesbian, for example, mean everyone has short hair, hates men, and drives (or rides on) a motorcycle? *What Does It Mean to Be Gay, Lesbian, Bisexual, or Transgender?* "smashes" these and other stereotypes.

Another common misconception is that "all gay people are alike"—a classic example of a stereotypical statement. We may be drawn together because of a common prejudice or oppression, but we should not forfeit our individuality for the sake of the safety of a common identity, which is one of the challenges shown in *Gay People of Color: Facing Prejudices, Forging Identities*.

Coming out to who *you* are is just as important as having a group or "family" within which to safely come out. Becoming knowledgeable about these issues (through the books in this series and the other resources to which they will lead), feeling good about yourself, behaving safely, actively listening to others *and* to your inner spirit—all this will allow you to fulfill your promise and potential.

James T. Sears, PhD
Consultant

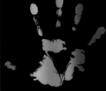

chapter 1

Is It Normal?

Historical records have shown that homosexuality has existed in various cultures around the globe for centuries. And the same question has been asked over and over again:

Is being gay normal?

That complicated question has been approached in many different ways. In the eleventh century, Saint Peter Damien introduced the term "sodomy." It was taken from the biblical story of Sodom, where the sinful behavior of the inhabitants led to the destruction of the city. The word became commonly used to refer to a particular type of sexual intercourse between two men. In Europe, and later in America, sodomy was considered a crime based on biblical law.

Medical and scientific issues related to homosexuality became more widespread in the nineteenth century, when German lawyer Karl Heinrich Ulrichs argued that homosexuality was an inherited biological

In the 1800s, Karl Heinrich Ulrichs was one of the first to speak out on behalf of gay rights.

condition and was not a matter of immorality. He was one of the first pioneers of gay civil rights, fighting against anti-sodomy laws in the late 1800s. Around that time, the word "homosexual" was introduced.

EXTRA INFO

Sigmund Freud believed all human beings started out life bisexual, and that they become heterosexual or homosexual as a result of their experiences with parents and others. Freud did not view a homosexual orientation a form of mental illness, but rather as simply a normal human option. In a now-famous letter to an American mother in 1935, Freud wrote:

> "Homosexuality is assuredly no advantage, but it is nothing to be ashamed of, no vice, no degradation, it cannot be classified as an illness. . . . Many highly respectable individuals of ancient and modern times have been homosexuals, several of the greatest men among them (Plato, Michelangelo, Leonardo da Vinci, etc.). It is a great injustice to persecute homosexuality as a crime, and cruelty too."

Sigmund Freud, considered the father of psycho-analysis, studied homosexuality at the beginning of the twentieth century. In the course of his research, he found that homosexuality could be the natural outcome of normal development. But after Freud's death, other researchers considered his theories flawed, and most medical professionals believed heterosexuality was the only natural human sexual development.

When the American Psychiatric Association first published the *Diagnostic and Statistical Manual of Mental Disorders* (DSM) in 1952, it listed homosexuality as a mental disorder. The DSM served as a tool to guide general psychiatric study, research, and treatment, but it also often reflected the **mainstream** cultural attitudes of the time.

What's That Mean?

Something that is *mainstream* is widely accepted by the majority of people.

A *deviation* is something abnormal, something that has moved away from the standard.

LGBT refers to lesbian, gay, bisexual, and transgender people; it is a catchall term to refer to this entire group of people.

The psychological concepts behind these studies and theories were very complicated. And as happens with all science, new information and technology provided information and answers that were never before available. Beginning in the 1940s, research on sexuality and mental health by Dr. Alfred Kinsey and psychologist Evelyn Hooker resulted in mounting evidence that homosexuality was *not* a mental disorder.

By the time the second edition of the DSM, known as DSM-II, was published in 1968, homosexuality was listed as a "sexual **deviation**," which was no longer categorized as a personality disturbance.

The following year, when a police raid on a gay bar prompted the historic Stonewall Riots in New York, the movement for gay civil rights began in full force. **LGBT** activists began to address the attitude of the American Psychiatric Association and specifically the presence of homosexuality in the DSM at all, regardless of the classification. By 1973, the American Psychiatric Association removed homosexuality

Sigmund Freud, the father of psychoanalysis, believed that homosexuality could be a part of normal development.

In 1953, Time *magazine honored Alfred Kinsey for his groundbreaking work on human sexuality. Thanks to Kinsey, people began to understand that homosexuality was not a mental disorder.*

from its list of mental disorders, and numerous other major medical organizations did the same.

Since then, the American Psychiatric Association has attempted to reverse some of the lasting effects the original DSM classification had on homosexual people. The organization has opposed employment *discrimination* based on *sexual orientation*, the dismissal of gay and lesbian people from the military, and medical treatments designed to "cure" someone of homosexuality.

As it has for centuries, the influence of the Bible and other religious texts and beliefs continues to lead some people to consider homosexuality to be immoral or sinful. Some claim that increased instances of mental health problems such as depression or substance abuse are more common in the LGBT community as a result of engaging in behavior that is wrong and harmful. But most scientific experts today agree that being gay is not an illness or a mental disorder, and instead, it is a natural occurrence in human sexual development.

What's That Mean?

Discrimination refers to treating people differently because of a certain characteristic about them, such as race, religion, or sexual orientation.

Sexual orientation is a phrase that describes a person's pattern of sexual attractions.

Imagine if you were a social outcast, simply because you liked strawberry ice cream while everyone else preferred vanilla!

Instead, the connection between identifying as lesbian, gay, bisexual, or transgender and potential mental health problems comes because of outside influences. Whatever the issue, when someone is subjected to **_harassment_** or abuse, it's only natural that the individual might encounter emotional challenges while dealing with such abuse!

"We tell people to think of it in terms of ice cream preferences," said Adrienne Hudek, a community educator on LGBT issues. "You like strawberry ice cream, but everyone else likes vanilla. And because of that, people are mean to you and make fun of you. They treat you badly, and maybe they even hurt you. Naturally, this is very upsetting to you. You get so upset, you need treatment from a mental health professional. Does that mean you were sick because you liked strawberry ice cream in the first place? Of course not. You became sick because of what the other people did to you, not because of who you are."

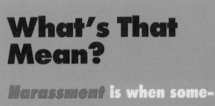

What's That Mean?

Harassment is when someone is continually bothered or tormented by another.

Promiscuity refers to having many sex partners on a casual basis.

Still, significant mental health issues do affect the LGBT community. Many do suffer from depression, and as a result fall victim to substance abuse, **_promiscuity_**, poor general health, and even suicide.

"This is an important distinction to make, because people look at the statistics and say, 'Wow, a lot of gay people are depressed or commit suicide. That just proves they were sick to begin with or that they shouldn't be gay.' But that's not the case at all," Hudek said. "There are millions of gay and lesbian people out there leading happy, healthy, and productive lives. But there are also some people who need a little bit of help to get there, and that's where mental health treatment comes in. There's absolutely nothing to be ashamed of and there's no reason to be afraid of help when you need it."

FIND OUT MORE ON THE INTERNET

Homosexuality: Facts for Teens
familydoctor.org/online/famdocen/home/children/teens/sexuality/739.html

StoneWall Society
www.stonewallsociety.com

READ MORE ABOUT IT

Huegel, Kelly. *GLBTQ: The Survival Guide for Queer and Questioning Teens.* Minneapolis, Minn.: Free Spirit Publishing, 2003.

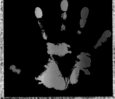

chapter 2

Depression and Suicide

When country singer Chely Wright was sixteen, she knew she was a lesbian. She was mostly comfortable with her identity inside, but she believed she could never show it on the outside.

"For the most part, I knew, I guess I'm okay. But I also knew—you have to hide this because I'm either going to get the crap beaten out of me or I'm going to get in big trouble," she said. "And I know I'm not going to fit in school. I know I'm not going to make it to the stage of the Opry. My band's not going to get hired. My dreams of country music wouldn't pan out."

As her career progressed, she had public relationships with men and kept her gay life hidden. For years, she struggled with trying to find happiness when she had to deny such an important part of herself. Even though she had commercial success, earning an Academy of Country Music Award and nominations for three Country Music Association

EXTRA INFO

The Grand Ole Opry is a weekly country music stage concert in Nashville, Tennessee, that has presented the biggest country musicians since 1925. Broadcast by WSM-AM, it is also the longest-running radio program in history. Dedicated to honoring country music and its history, the Opry showcases a mix of legends and contemporary chart-toppers performing country, bluegrass, folk, comedy, and gospel. Considered an American icon, it attracts hundreds of thousands of visitors from around the world and millions of radio and Internet listeners. The Opry, today part of the American landscape, is "the show that made country music famous," and it has also been called the "home of American music." With it's conservative, all-American, gospel connections, the Opry has not been known for openly welcoming gays.

Awards, she was depressed about the piece of her life that was missing.

Then, when she was in her mid-thirties, she found herself standing in her home, staring at herself in the mirror. She had a gun in her mouth, and she was ready to pull the trigger.

"At that moment, I was looking at myself and feeling like I was outside of my body, watching somebody do something that I had made such a harsh

Country singer Chely Wright struggled with depression and suicidal feelings until she finally accepted and acknowledged her gay identity.

judgment about my entire life," she said. "I had been so critical of people who had committed suicide; I judged them for being God-less and weak. And I was watching that in the mirror and realizing, 'Holy crap! That's me.'

"But as I was about to pull the trigger, I realized I wasn't crying. And I was shocked: Shouldn't I be crying? Don't people cry when they kill themselves? Isn't it supposed to be more emotional than this?

"And as I was about to pull my thumb back and do it, I said a prayer to God to forgive me for what I was about to do because I know the gift of life is the most precious thing. And I had some things in my life that kind of flashed through my brain and one of them was sunlight and I thought about my dogs and I thought about music and how much I love music. And I thought about a kiss from my partner, my ex-partner—the only love in my life I'd ever known—and I heard a noise and it was the sound of my heart pounding in my head.

"And I looked up in the mirror again and my eyes were just welled up with tears and my cheeks were wet and tears were streaming down. I could barely even see. I couldn't focus because there were so many tears coming out of my eyes. And the dam broke. And my emotions enveloped me and I became one with myself again. I got back into my body. I was no longer outside of my body watching this cold person—this human with a gun in her mouth. I didn't know that I wasn't going to—on the next day—kill myself. I knew on that night I wouldn't do it."

Wright was never tempted to take such a drastic action again, and instead she began to accept who she really was. She decided to come out publicly in 2010, a move that she believes set her free and gave her a sort of re-birth in her life.

For thousands of lesbian, gay, bisexual, and transgender (LGBT) people, suicide seems like the only option when they are faced with the immense struggles and stress of understanding and accepting their sexual orientation.

As part of the normal experience of growing up, many teenagers encounter significant feelings of stress, confusion and self-doubt. These intense feelings can be overwhelming for anyone, which is why suicide is the third leading cause of death among young people ages fifteen to twenty-four. And these emotions are often much more challenging for LGBT youth, especially if they don't have the resources or support necessary to help them. Studies have shown that LGBT young people who do not receive support from their families are more than eight times more likely to attempt suicide than their straight peers.

Much research has been done to determine exactly why this is the case. The increased number of suicide attempts among LGBT people is not because of their sexual orientation itself. In other words, feeling suicidal is not part of being gay or the result of coming

Today, Chely Wright feels she has experienced a rebirth, knowing that she is accepted by both God and herself.

out. Instead, these feelings can come as a response to being bullied at school, being treated poorly at home or in a religious community, or feeling as if they have failed to live up to expectations of being "normal."

"Families and caregivers have a dramatic and compelling impact on their LGBT children's health, mental health, and well-being," said Caitlin Ryan, director of the Family Acceptance Project, who works with parents of LGBT children. "We tell parents and families that they need to provide a supportive environment for their children before they know who they'll become."

Being gay or lesbian isn't something individuals can control or change. So when LGBT people hear their friends or families make jokes about other gay people, it can have a strong and lasting impression. Likewise, when people questioning their sexuality believe that others will not accept them if they are gay, they are more inclined to hide their feelings.

When anyone is told they are bad or wrong because of who they are, that trauma and stress can lead to mental health issues such as depression or anxiety. This is frequently what happens to LGBT people and others who are considered different from their peers, putting them at risk for suicide.

Depression is a medical condition. Individuals suffering from depression may constantly feel sad or tense.

"At first I was feeling sad all the time, even though I had no reason to be," said Rob, who shared his experience with depression on the resource website 4therapy.com. "Then the sadness turned into anger, and I started having fights with my family and friends. I felt really bad about myself, like I wasn't good enough for anyone. It got so bad that I wished I would go to bed and never wake up."

People struggling with depression often lose energy and feel restless or tired all the time. In some cases, this can lead to thinking that suicide is the only option or the only way to fix a very difficult situation.

"Teens need to know that they can go to their parents with a problem and their parents won't hate them or hit them and they could talk it through," said Ryan.

Parents, family members, and friends also need to be able to recognize the signs of depression. In Rob's case, his brother noticed that his behavior changed and immediately suggested that Rob see a doctor. Rob did, and he learned that depression is a real illness. It's not something that can be fixed by being told to "cheer up" and be happy. Like all medical problems, the most effective treatment will come from a doctor or other health care professional. Rob began seeing a therapist, who helped him talk through his problems.

"This treatment helps me control depression in my everyday life," he said. "It has taken some time, but I'm finally feeling like myself again."

People who don't understand that depression is an illness often seek cures or treatments that may seem to work in the short term by dulling the pain—such

All teens experience times of depression and loneliness. When feelings of sadness and isolation become overwhelming, however, to the point that they interfere with a person's ability to live life, that person needs help from a psychologist or psychiatrist.

If a gay teen is told that being homosexual is an illness or a sin, it becomes even harder for him to come to terms with his identity. Trying to cope with his feelings of rejection and loneliness can trigger depression and other mental-health issues

as drugs or alcohol—but that won't provide the real support and attention that individuals suffering from depression actually need. In fact, alcohol itself is a depressant; in the long run, it just makes people who are depressed feel even worse.

In a similar way, when parents, friends and other family members don't understand what it means to be LGBT, they often look for some type of treatment or cure that will make people straight. While people may be able to change the way they behave, experts explain that a person's identity on the inside isn't something that can be removed or made different. And often attempting to do this can do much more harm than good.

"If kids get the message that who they are is unacceptable, then they will carry that scar for the rest of their lives," said Gary Remafedi, a professor of pediatrics at University of Minnesota. "Telling parents that this is an illness, that they should force their children to seek some cure that doesn't exist, is *quackery* and it's *malpractice*."

What's That Mean?

Quackery is when an untrained person gives medical advice or treatment, pretending to be a doctor or other medical expert.

Malpractice is when a doctor or other professional gives bad advice or treatment, either because of ignorance, negligence, or on purpose.

Gay teens who feel that their identities are not accepted are more likely to struggle with alcohol abuse.

All this also can increase feelings of depression and isolation. When people reach the point of feeling hopeless enough to consider suicide, there are often outward signs and indicators. They may see themselves as bad or inferior people and tell their friends about those feelings. Suicidal teens may also withdraw from their friends, spend time alone, abuse drugs and alcohol, and lose interest in things they usually enjoy.

Any statements a person makes that suggest she may be considering suicide should always be taken seriously. Sometimes just talking about the issues—whether with a parent, friend, or mental health professional—can be very helpful. The key is to not ignore these feeling and to seek help as soon as possible.

"Suicide is truly a permanent solution to a temporary problem," said Ashley Albright, who works for a suicide prevention program. "Although we can give you the number of completed and attempted suicides throughout the past decade, there is no way we can give how many times someone took the opportunity to listen, care—and a life was saved."

FIND OUT MORE ON THE INTERNET

Depression and GLBT Issues
www.healthyplace.com/gender/depression-and-gender/
depression-and-glbt-issues/menu-id-585/

Suicide and the GLBT Community
www.soulforce.org/article/653

READ MORE ABOUT IT

Gold, Mitchell, and Mindy Drucker, eds. *Crisis: 40 Stories Revealing the Personal, Social, and Religious Pain and Trauma of Growing Up Gay in America.* Austin, Texas: Greenleaf Book Group, 2008.

Hardin, Kimeron, and Marny Hall. *Queer Blues: The Lesbian and Gay Guide to Overcoming Depression.* Oakland, Calif.: New Harbinger Publications, 2001.

chapter 3

Self-Esteem

When Anna Rangos walked down the halls of her high school, she frequently heard *homophobic* slurs from her classmates. Eventually, it became so bad that she brought the issue to her district's school board in May 2010.

"My self-esteem just totally dropped because of what was being said. Every single year, there's an incident, and I've never seen a kid punished," she said. "After a while, it's so frustrating, it hurts a lot to have people say those things to you while not having people who are supposed to protect you do that."

In most American high schools, bullying isn't limited to lesbian, gay, bisexual, and transgender students. According to the National Center for

What's That Mean?

Homophobic means showing fear or hatred of homo-sexuals.

Bullying is a fact of life for about a third of all adolescents.

Educational Statistics, about one in three students (about one-third or 30 percent) between the ages of twelve and eighteen reported being bullied in school in 2009. Eight years earlier, only 14 percent of that population said they had experienced bullying.

But for LGBT students, this type of harassment can be even more damaging because it reinforces feelings of confusion or loneliness they may already have because they are different from most of their classmates.

Bullying has been cited as a probable contributor to many teen suicides, including high-profile cases in 2009 involving students as young as eleven years old. This has led to a heightened awareness for educators and parents about the effects of bullying.

"This is going to give a whole new complexion to bullying and prevention here in the United States," said Marlene Snyder, director of development for an anti-bullying program used in many American high schools. "The message that needs to get out is you need to pay attention to what the kids are doing and there are programs out there that can help."

At Rangos's high school, there is a Gay-Straight Alliance. But she said many of her classmates didn't participate in the group because they were afraid of being labeled and harassed by other students. When she listened to the way other students in her school spoke, she often heard anti-gay statements that made her feel bad about herself, even when that may not have been the intention.

"When you use the phrase 'That's so gay,' it may not seem harmful, but it still does hurt inside," she said.

That common line is often used as a slang way to say something is weird or strange. Though it is often used by people who don't think about its true meaning, what it is really saying is that being gay is wrong and negative. When someone hears that over and over, they can begin to think it's true.

That can lead to something called *internalized* homophobia—when LGBT people think negatively about themselves and their lives because of all the bad things they hear other people say about gay people. This often keeps LGBT people from coming out, and instead they feel the need to keep their sexual orientation a secret. In many cases, they may even actively try to hide who they are because they are afraid.

"When I first got to Nashville . . . I worked at a theme park called Opryland and there were gay boys

What's That Mean?

Something that is *internalized* is taken into yourself and made a part of your attitudes and beliefs.

An *abomination* is a horrible, disgusting, and hated action or thing.

in my cast," said gay country singer Chely Wright. "I don't know that there were any gay girls. But I was fully aware that I was gay, of course, and I was very sure that God was okay with me. Yet I slung daggers of hatred toward the gay boys because I was so afraid that they might identify something in me that would be some identifying factor—that they might be able to know that I was gay and I wanted to throw them off in case they thought I might be."

That reaction is not at all uncommon, especially among people like Wright who have strong religious beliefs. She told the boys they were an ***abomination***, and that what they did was disgusting. These were the messages that she had heard from her church and other people in her life.

As Wright got older and understood more about herself, she saw that this was her own internalized homophobia. She was so frightened of other people's reaction to her that she attacked other people who were like her. After she came out, she said this was something she strongly regretted.

"When I would go into Tower Records in Nashville, I was recognized by the young kids that worked at the record store," she said. "In fact, they would bring records or posters for me to sign. And I was a fan of kd lang's music. But when she came out, I wouldn't purchase a kd lang or Melissa Etheridge [another openly gay musician] record in Nashville because I

Self-image can be a fragile thing. If you constantly hear that your identity is bad or abnormal, it will be hard for you to see who you really are.

was afraid for them to see me buying it. That comes with a great deal of shame for me to admit. I'm embarrassed to admit that— but that's how deep the fear and pain went."

When a fellow singer asked Wright directly if she was gay, she denied it. In that moment, she realized something in her life had to change. She didn't believe that being gay was a sin, but she believed that lying was. And for the first time, instead of just hiding who she was, she had clearly lied about it.

This helped her decide to come out to the world in 2010. She didn't want to be one of those people who said one thing in public, but did something else in their real lives. She recognized that same behavior in other high-profile people, such as politicians and religious leaders, who would publicly **demonize** the LGBT community, while privately they were actually gay.

"I felt it was really important for me to stand up and admit that because it *is* so **prevalent** in our culture, in American society," she said. "Because we've got people writing legislation and people in public office, people in powerful positions who have the chance

"Coming out of the closet" is the term gays use for revealing their true identities to their friends and families. It takes courage to face others' opinions about something so intimate—but the more people who take this step, the more the rest of the world will recognize and respect the LGBT community.

and the opportunity to write policy who are signing paperwork that goes against the gay community and they themselves are *closeted.* And I thought it was really important that I say, 'Pay attention to those who are the most vocal against gays and lesbians because I can tell you—those who spew the most venom, pay attention to that.' Because I did it."

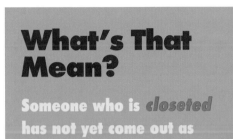

What's That Mean?

Someone who is *closeted* has not yet come out as being gay.

While some people may turn their personal confusion or self-hatred toward people who are like them, others may allow themselves to be in dangerous or abusive situations. A 2010 study by the University of California Los Angeles (UCLA) showed that 27.9 percent of the gay and lesbian adults and 40.6 percent of bisexual adults reported intimate partner violence. That is violence committed by a husband, wife, boyfriend, girlfriend, or lover. The numbers for gay, lesbian, and bisexual people were significantly higher than straight couples, of which only 16.7 percent reported incidences of intimate partner violence.

This doesn't meant that LGBT people are more abusive than straight people. But it does mean that LGBT are more willing to put up with abusive relationships than straight people are. Often, this is because they lack the self-esteem they need to protect themselves.

"Gays, lesbians, and bisexuals still face discrimination on a number of fronts," said Dr. Elaine Zahnd, one of the lead researchers who worked on the UCLA study. "Some heterosexuals seek to **stigmatize** and isolate gays, lesbians, and bisexuals. Stigma and social isolation may result in lower self-esteem and increase one's **vulnerability** to abuse."

Zahnd's research team also found that nearly one in ten people who reported violence in their relationships also engaged in binge drinking. This is most likely a way to cope with the abuse, which many people feel they deserve, because they think of themselves as being worthless or hopeless.

What's That Mean?

Stigmatize means to characterize as shameful and disgraceful.

Vulnerability means being open to attack and capable of being hurt.

"Self-medication to deal with stigma and discrimination may result in risky alcohol or drug use," she said. "Both mental and emotional health problems and risky alcohol and drug use have been shown to be associated with violent victimization. [In the study,] about one-third of the violence was associated with substance use. It may be to mask the pain, or it may occur in situations where mutual fighting or battering takes place."

Substance abuse is a significant health issue in the LGBT community. Excessive use of alcohol and drugs

EXTRA INFO

In many places around the world, including the United States, people think that HIV/AIDS is a "gay disease." People who have HIV/AIDS are sometimes rejected and discriminated against; some have lost their jobs or been the victims of violence. The stigma that's been attached to HIV/AIDS has kept many people from seeking HIV testing—or from being treated, once they've received a diagnosis. This can turn what might otherwise being a manageable chronic disease into a death sentence.

In many developed countries, there is an association between AIDS and homosexuality or bisexuality, and this association goes along with higher levels of homosexual prejudice. However, in the developing world, such as many nations in Africa, HIV/AIDS is more common among heterosexuals. This is because risky sexual behaviors, whether heterosexual or homosexual, put you at risk of getting HIV/AIDS.

can lead to making wrong decisions and even more risky behavior, such as unprotected sex. That can put people at risk of contracting sexually transmitted diseases, including HIV, the virus that causes AIDS. Again, making the choice to use drugs or have unsafe sex is the result of issues related to poor self-esteem and low feelings of self-worth. These behaviors don't have anything to do with being gay in and of itself!

When a person feels that he is wrong, sinful, or worthless because he's gay, he may not feel that it's important to take care of his health or to protect himself from sexually transmitted diseases. He may also use drugs and alcohol to take away those feelings of sadness and depression. But that never really makes those feelings go away entirely. It just hides them for a little while. Over time, it may take more alcohol or harder drugs to keep those feelings buried, and that is the way many people become addicted to drugs and alcohol.

"It happens all the time, and it becomes so familiar that you can almost see it coming a mile away," said Adrienne Hudek, who works with at-risk youth

Family rejection during adolescence can affect a person's adult life, making her more vulnerable to depression and suicidal feelings.

in the LGBT community. "A guy who's barely even out of the closet yet goes to a gay club and maybe he tries drugs or alcohol. And for the first time in probably a very long time, he feels good. He feels happy. The drugs make him forget about everything that's challenging in his life. He doesn't feel bad about who he is anymore. So when he goes home and mom or dad tells him he's a sinner, or when kids at school threaten him and call him names, he remembers how good the drugs felt. He'll think about how great that was, compared to how bad his real life is. So he'll want to do them again, because it makes it easier to deal with the pain and shame that he feels every day. But it doesn't really work out that way."

Researchers at the Family Acceptance Project at San Francisco State University studied the impact of rejection or acceptance of LGBT people by their families. What the researchers found was that the people who reported high levels of rejection from their families during adolescence were eight times more likely to have attempted suicide by age twenty-five. They were also nearly six times more likely to have serious issues with depression, and their risk for drug abuse and contracting sexually transmitted diseases was three times higher than the overall population.

"That just shows how serious and damaging it can be when kids feel like they have nowhere to turn," Hudek said. "The most effective way to stop this is to let kids know that there is help available to them. It's never easy. And no matter how they make someone feel at the time, drugs and alcohol make this so much worse, not better."

FIND OUT MORE ON THE INTERNET

Live Out Loud
www.liveoutloud.info

READ MORE ABOUT IT

Hardin, Kimeron. *Loving Ourselves: The Gay and Lesbian Guide to Self-Esteem*. New York: Alyson Books, 2008.

Pimental-Habib, Richard. *Empowering the Tribe: A Positive Guide to Gay and Lesbian Self-Esteem*. New York: Kensington, 2008.

chapter 4
Getting Help

In 1994, Peggy Rajski and Randy Stone won an Academy Award for their short film, *Trevor*, the story of a gay thirteen-year-old boy who attempted to kill himself after being rejected by his loved ones. A few years later, when the film was scheduled to be aired on television, Rajski and Stone realized that some people watching it might be struggling with the same issues. They realized they needed to provide some information on suicide prevention resources for lesbian, gay, bisexual, and transgender teenagers. So they began to look for a telephone number or other contact information that could be provided.

They couldn't find any.

Rajski and Stone were so disturbed by that discovery that they created the Trevor Project, a nonprofit organization that features a twenty-four-hour crisis and suicide prevention telephone helpline available to people who need help and feel they have no place else to turn. Now it also includes a website that

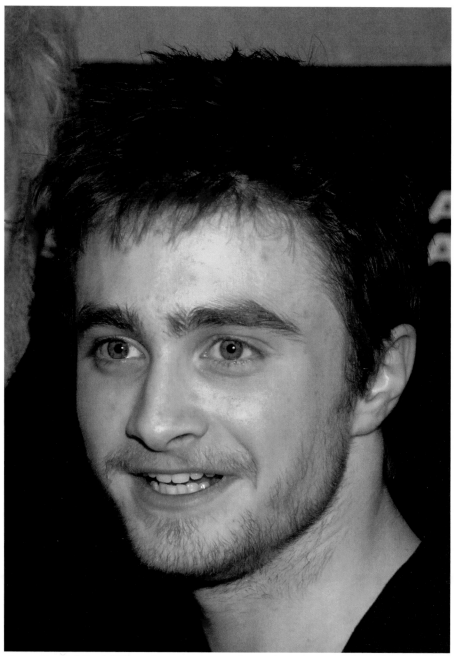

Actor Daniel Radcliffe, of Harry Potter fame, has spoken out against homophobia

provides information to help parents and educators support LGBT young people.

"I grew up knowing a lot of gay men and it was never something that I even thought twice about—that some men were gay and some weren't," said British actor Daniel Radcliffe, best known for his portrayal as Harry Potter in the blockbuster movie franchise. "And then I went to school and for the first time . . . I came across homophobia. . . . I had never encountered it before. It shocked me. I have always hated anybody who is not tolerant of gay men or lesbians or bisexuals."

In 2010, Radcliffe became one in a string of high-profile people who have supported the Trevor Project, which he learned about while performing on Broadway in the United States. He also contributed by bringing more attention to the issue of LGBT teen suicide with a Public Service Announcement.

"I think it's important for somebody from a big, commercial movie series like Harry Potter [to support the Trevor Project] and particularly because I am not gay or bisexual or transgendered," Radcliffe said. "The fact that I am straight makes not a difference, but it shows that straight people are incredibly interested and care a lot about this as well."

Though the Trevor Project was founded to provide resources for LGBT youth who are considering suicide, it also provides information to help them deal

Talking with a counselor or therapist gives you safe place to be open about your private feelings and identity.

with issues before they reach such an extreme point. The website offers the Ask Trevor page, where visitors can send confidential questions about issues of sexual orientation and identity. Trained counselors then supply answers and assist with finding additional resources that can be helpful, covering everything from coming out to relationships to helping young people figure out whether or not they're gay. The site also features past letters from other visitors, along with their responses. The site provides information to people who want to support family or friends who are LGBT or who are questioning their sexuality.

Issues of identity are challenging for everyone, and answering those questions isn't simple. In fact, it's impossible for anyone to define someone else's sexual orientation. It's a personal issue, and one that people must work through and understand on their own.

"I've been asked so many times, 'how do I know if I'm gay?'" said Adrienne Hudek, who helps connect LGBT people with mental health resources and support groups. "People will list off a bunch of things they do or say or think. And then they ask if that makes them gay. But it's not that simple. It's not something somebody else can tell you or answer for you. You have to answer it for yourself. But there are people out there who can help."

This can be especially confusing for someone to try sort through alone, Hudek said. And many young people are unwilling to discuss issues of sexual identity with someone else. While some may be worried about homophobia or rejection, others may just be embarrassed to discuss the many personal topics related to sexuality. That's why the confidentiality and ***anonymity*** of the Internet can be a very helpful resource for anyone questioning his or her sexual orientation.

The Internet offers teens a way to connect with others, anywhere, any time. Be careful to follow Internet safety rules, however.

"Plenty of people have questions and they don't feel comfortable asking a stranger, whether it's a social worker, counselor, or doctor," Hudek said. "That makes sense, because these can be very personal conversations. So we recommend some excellent websites that give some terrific, *credible* information. And the good part of that is, you really see that you're not alone. People all over the world are asking the same questions and dealing with the same issues."

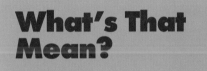

What's That Mean?

Anonymity means being unknown, having no one know who you are.

Something that is *credible* is believable and reliable.

In addition to the Trevor Project, other websites like Go Ask Alice! can provide helpful information and insight. Go Ask Alice! is a health question-and-answer service produced by Columbia University. It includes a wide range of health information about topics such as acne, fertility, aromatherapy, fitness, tattoo safety, and much more. And it provides guidance on LGBT issues, such as how to identify one's own orientation. For example, a reader asked about her possible bisexual feelings and received this response:

We are often called to label ourselves as purely sexually inclined one way or the other, either to be attracted to guys or to girls only, end of story. But in actuality, most people fall somewhere on a spectrum of attraction, fantasy, desire, and action with people of all genders. The curiosity your friend has sparked in you could be just that—same-gender wonderings— or it could be the *impetus* for discovering that you are bisexual, and may be attracted to other women in the future.

The pioneering sex researcher Alfred Kinsey broke from popular thinking on sexuality in the 1950s, theorizing that bisexuality was in fact far more common than previously thought. Kinsey is perhaps most famous for his sexual-orientation scale, which represents exclusive heterosexuality with a zero and exclusive homosexuality with a six—bisexuality is regarded as an approximate three, when a person is equally attracted to or has had sexual experiences (including fantasies) with both men and women.

Most humans experience erotic desires, act on those desires, and have relationships in a social context. Kinsey's research showed that bisexuals had more sexual experiences with one gender or another

What's That Mean?

Impetus is something that causes or starts an action

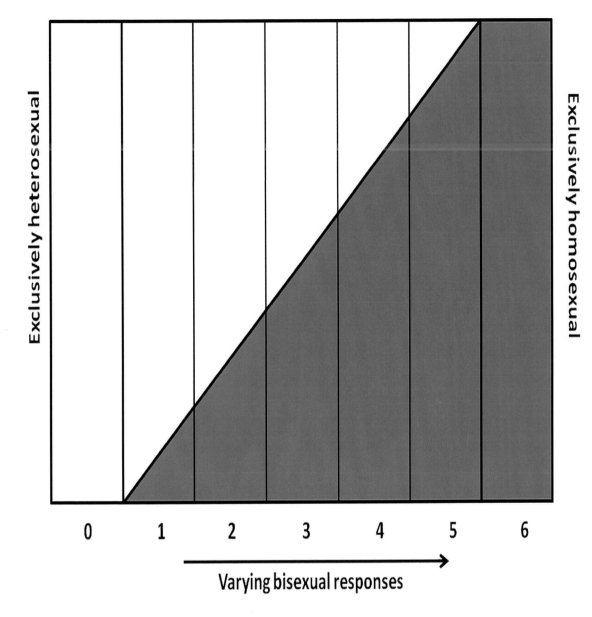

Exclusively heterosexual

Exclusively homosexual

0   1   2   3   4   5   6

Varying bisexual responses

The Kinsey Scale portrayed sexual attraction and orientation as a spectrum, along which many individuals would fall somewhere between exclusively heterosexual and exclusively homosexual.

depending on their social environment. In other words, factors that we might not think of as sexual per se, like political and social ties, can in fact influence those who we choose to be with and whether we identify ourselves as straight, gay, bi, queer, etc.

The development of sexual orientation occurs throughout youth and adolescence. Studies show that young people, gay or straight, first become aware of sexual attraction by about age twelve. As they develop, many young people experiment with sexual activity. According to the American Academy of Pediatrics, a survey of thirteen- to nineteen-year-olds found that one in ten boys and one in seventeen girls reported having at least one same-sex sexual experience; but most studies estimate that only 2 percent to 7 percent of U.S. teens consider themselves lesbian, gay, or bisexual.

"By the time children are eleven, twelve, and thirteen, they have a very good sense that their sexual orientation may be different from the majority of their friends," said Ellen Perrin, a developmental-behavioral pediatrician at the Floating Hospital for Children at Tufts Medical Center in Boston. "There is no evidence that people could become gay because of external influences."

That's why talking about these issues can be so helpful. Other people have likely had the same experiences, questions and concerns. The Gay and Lesbian National Hotline provides trained peer counselors who can help young people discuss their feelings and questions in a productive, nonjudgmental way. While there isn't always an easy way for people to answer questions about themselves, these resources can help.

Many people struggling with LGBT issues are often conflicted because of their religious beliefs. Some religions teach that being gay is a sin, and that sinners won't get to heaven. They may even use the Bible to support ideas that are intolerant of LGBT people. It becomes difficult, then, for religious people to accept and embrace their sexual orientation if it will result in such terrible consequences. Many people don't want to risk coming out if it means losing their religious foundation and being separated from their spiritual values.

But there are millions of LGBT people around the world who remain devoted to their religions while still accepting and loving themselves and their sexual orientation. The Al-Fatiha Foundation supports Muslims of all cultures who are LGBT. And there are several denominations in Judaism, including Progressive and Reform Judaism, which accept and welcome gay and lesbian members. DignityUSA is an organization for LGBT Catholics, and there are hundreds of other gay-inclusive churches and Christian organizations throughout the United States.

Not all churches reject homosexuals. Churches that display the Rainbow Flag proclaim their welcome to people in the LGBT community.

In 2010, Grammy-nominated Christian singer Jennifer Knapp grabbed attention in the Christian community when she came out publicly. Though some were upset and disappointed by this, she also received a lot of support. Religious leaders are also optimistic that as more role models emerge, people will recognize that it is possible to be both gay and committed to your faith.

"A lot of youth are suicidal over their realization of their own sexuality," said Justin Lee, executive director of the Gay Christian Network, a nonprofit *ministry* in Raleigh, North Carolina. "The *dichotomy* will continue in the church, but with high-profile artists coming out, we'll see the church reevaluate how it addresses these issues."

Considering all of the reasons some people may have to be afraid, it's important to remember that simply ignoring the issue of sexual identity won't make it go away. That fear and uncertainty will remain, and it can turn into something that can be very damaging.

When someone is questioning her sexual orientation, the healthiest thing to do is to seek information

What's That Mean?

A *ministry* is a religious group or organization that works to help others in a certain way.

A *dichotomy* is a division into two opposite and contradictory groups.

and answers. Finding supportive family members, friends, or mental health professionals can help people feel safe and secure as they work through their questions. If that's not an option, then speaking with a trained hotline counselor can be the next-best alternative.

"No one can tell you if you're gay, lesbian, bisexual, or straight, and nobody ever should," said Adrienne Hudek, who also counsels young people who are questioning their sexuality. "The purpose of these services isn't to convince someone that they're gay. We know that's not even possible. What we do is provide a safe and confidential way for people to be able to talk about things they might otherwise keep hidden inside, where they can really do damage. We talk openly and honestly about how people feel, so they can make healthy choices that are right for them."

FIND OUT MORE ON THE INTERNET

GLBT National Help Center
www.glnh.org

The Trevor Project
www.thetrevorproject.org

READ MORE ABOUT IT

Belge, Kathy, and Marke Bieschke. *Queer: The Ultimate LGBT Guide for Teens.* San Francisco, Calif.: Zest, 2010.

D'Angelo, Anthony J., Stephen D. Collingsworth, Jr., Mike Esposito, Gabriel Hermelin, Ronni Sanlo, Lydia A. Sausa, and Shane L. Windmeyer. *Inspiration for LGBT Students and Their Allies.* Easton, Penn.: The Collegiate EmPowerment Company, 2002.

BIBLIOGRAPHY

Al-Fatiha Foundation, www.al-fatiha.org (18 May 2010)

Beck, Melinda. "What to Say When Your Teenager Says She's Gay." *The Wall Street Journal*, 11 May 2010.

De Arcangelis, Alessandro. "Harry Potter Hero Daniel Radcliffe Backs The Trevor Project." *News Blaze,* 5 March 2010.

DiFilippo, Dana. "Experts Puzzled, Worried by Youngsters' Suicides." *Philadelphia Daily News,* 16 May 2010.

Echegaray, Chris. "Christian Star Jennifer Knapp Lets Go, Comes Out." *The Tennessean,* 9 May 2010.

Kennedy, Hubert. *Karl Heinrich Ulrichs: Pioneer of the Modern Gay Movement*. Concord, Calif.: Peremptory Publications, 2002.

Ocamb, Karen. "Country Star Chely Wright Comes Out, Talks About Suicide, God, Melissa, kd and the Indigo Girls." *The Huffington Post,* 6 May 2010.

Ollove, Michael. "Bullying and Teen Suicide: How Do We Adjust School Climate?" *Christian Science Monitor,* 28 April 2010.

"Student Seeks Greater Consequences for Harassment of Gay Students." *Niles Herald-Spectator,* 10 May 2010.

"Teen Suicide." *American Academy of Child & Adolescent Psychiatry*, May 2008.

The Trevor Project. www.thetrevorproject.org (17 May 2010).

Zahnd, Elaine, et all. "Nearly Four Million California Adults Are Victims of Intimate Partner Violence." UCLA Center for Health Policy Research, April 2010.

INDEX

ABOUT THE AUTHOR AND THE CONSULTANT

Jaime A. Seba's involvement in LGBT issues began in 2004, when she helped open the doors of the Pride Center of Western New York, which served a community of more than 100,000 people. As head of public education and outreach, she spearheaded one of the East Coast's first crystal methamphetamine awareness and harm reduction campaigns. She also wrote and developed successful grant programs through the Susan G. Komen Breast Cancer Foundation, securing funding for the region's first breast cancer prevention program designed specifically for gay, bisexual, and transgender women. Jaime studied political science at Syracuse University before switching her focus to communications with a journalism internship at the Press & Sun-Bulletin in Binghamton, New York, in 1999. She is currently a freelance writer based in Seattle.

James T. Sears specializes in research in lesbian, gay, bisexual, and transgender issues in education, curriculum studies, and queer history. His scholarship has appeared in a variety of peer-reviewed journals and he is the author or editor of twenty books and is the Editor of the *Journal of LGBT Youth*. Dr. Sears has taught curriculum, research, and LGBT-themed courses in the departments of education, sociology, women's studies, and the honors college at several universities, including: Trinity University, Indiana University, Harvard University, Penn State University, the College of Charleston, and the University of South Carolina. He has also been a Research Fellow at Center for Feminist Studies at the University of Southern California, a Fulbright Senior Research Southeast Asia Scholar on sexuality and culture, a Research Fellow at the University of Queensland, a consultant for the J. Paul Getty Center for Education and the Arts, and a Visiting Research Lecturer in Brazil. He lectures throughout the world.